W9-APO-891

Roseate Spoonbill

by Ellen Lawrence

Consultant:

Bryan P. Piazza, PhD
Director, Freshwater and Marine Science
The Nature Conservancy, Louisiana Chapter
Baton Rouge, Louisiana

BEARPORT PUBLISHING

New York, New York

McLEAN MERCER REGIONAL LIBRARY
BOX 505
RIVERDALE, ND 58565

Credits
Cover, © Arto Hakola/Shutterstock; 4, © John Zada/Alamy; 5, © Robert Bannister/Alamy; 6, © Cosmographics; 7, © Jill Nightingale/Shutterstock; 8, © Agustin Esmoris/Shutterstock; 9, © Bonnie Taylor Barry/Shutterstock; 10, © Arto Hakola/Shutterstock; 11TL, © Dmitrijs Mihejevs/Shutterstock; 11TR, © Bradford Lumley/Dreamstime; 11B, © Eric Olsen/FLPA; 12, © Ernie Janes/Alamy; 13, © G Talley/Shutterstock; 14, © Ivan Kuzmin/Shutterstock; 15, © mark smith nsb/Shutterstock; 16, © Dan Guravich/Science Source/Ardea; 17, © Clark 42/IstockPhoto; 18, © Bonnie Taylor Barry/Shutterstock; 19TL, © Steve Byland/Shutterstock; 19TR, © Miroslav Hlavako/Shutterstock; 19B, © Keneva Photography/Shutterstock; 20, © Bonnie Taylor Barry/Shutterstock; 21, © Bildagentur Zoonar GmbH/Shutterstock; 22L, © Bonnie Taylor Barry/Shutterstock; 22R, © Steven Russell Smith Photos/Shutterstock; 23TL, © Melissa Faith Knight/Shutterstock; 23TC, © Arto Hakola/Shutterstock; 23TR, © bikeriderlondon/Shutterstock; 23BL, © Steve Bower/Shutterstock; 23BC, © Ivan Kuzmin/Shutterstock; 23BR, © Martha Marks/Shutterstock.

Publisher: Kenn Goin
Editor: Jessica Rudolph
Creative Director: Spencer Brinker
Design: Emma Randall
Photo Researcher: Ruby Tuesday Books Ltd

Library of Congress Cataloging-in-Publication Data

Names: Lawrence, Ellen, 1967– author.
Title: Roseate spoonbill / by Ellen Lawrence.
Description: New York, New York : Bearport Publishing, [2017] | Series: Swamp
  things: animal life in a wetland | Audience: Ages 7–11._ | Includes
  bibliographical references and index.
Identifiers: LCCN 2016012271 (print) | LCCN 2016013195 (ebook) | ISBN
  9781944102531 (library binding) | ISBN 9781944997212 (ebook)
Subjects: LCSH: Roseate spoonbill—Juvenile literature. | Swamp
  animals—Juvenile literature. | Swamp ecology—Juvenile literature.
Classification: LCC QL696.C585 L39 2017 (print) | LCC QL696.C585 (ebook) |
  DDC 598.3/4—dc23
LC record available at http://lccn.loc.gov/2016012271

Copyright © 2017 Bearport Publishing Company, Inc. All rights reserved. No part of this publication may be reproduced in whole or in part, stored in any retrieval system, or transmitted in any form or by any means, electronic, mechanical, photocopying, recording, or otherwise, without written permission from the publisher.

For more information, write to Bearport Publishing Company, Inc., 45 West 21st Street, Suite 3B, New York, New York 10010. Printed in the United States of America.

10 9 8 7 6 5 4 3 2 1

Contents

Morning in the Swamp

It's early morning in the Atchafalaya (*uh*-chaf-uh-LYE-uh) **Swamp**.

The sun shines through the tall trees onto a **shallow** lake.

A large bird with white, pink, and red feathers is walking slowly through the water.

The bird is a roseate spoonbill, and the swamp is its home.

the Atchafalaya Swamp

Roseate spoonbills are **wading** birds. Their long legs help them move, or wade, through water.

roseate spoonbill

A Roseate Spoonbill's World

Roseate spoonbills live in North and South America.

They often make their homes in swampy areas like the Atchafalaya.

A swamp is a type of **wetland**.

In swamps, much of the land is covered with shallow water.

Trees and bushes grow from the water-covered land.

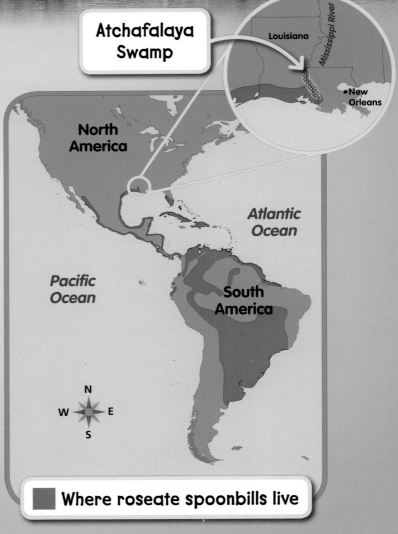

Atchafalaya Swamp

Louisiana

Mississippi River

New Orleans

North America

Atlantic Ocean

Pacific Ocean

South America

N W E S

Where roseate spoonbills live

Roseate spoonbills also live in marshes, which are another kind of wetland. Grasses and other low-growing plants are found in marshes.

a roseate spoonbill in a marsh

How do you think the roseate spoonbill got its name?

7

Meet a Roseate Spoonbill

The roseate spoonbill has a long, flat **bill**.

Its body is covered with feathers, but its head is bald.

The colorful bird has pink legs and bright red eyes.

It's also very big—about 2.5 feet (0.8 m) tall.

When the bird spreads its wings, they measure about 4 feet (1.2 m) across.

bill

The roseate spoonbill gets the first part of its name from its color. *Rose* means "pink." The bird is called a spoonbill because its bill is shaped like a flat spoon.

How do you think the bird uses its bill to find food?

Wading for a Meal

How does a roseate spoonbill find food in the swamp?

It dips its open bill into the water.

Then, as the spoonbill wades, it swings its head from side to side.

It feels for small fish, shrimp, and insects under the water.

When the bird finds food, it snaps its bill shut and grabs the meal.

a spoonbill hunting for food

10

minnow

shrimp

a spoonbill eating a fish

The bird's bill can feel the tiniest movement of an animal under the water. Hunting by touch is helpful in swamps, where the water is often muddy and dark.

Swamp Neighbors

Roseate spoonbills live in large groups called colonies.

A colony may include hundreds of birds.

Spoonbills share their watery home with other wading birds.

Storks, herons, and egrets often live in spoonbill colonies.

The birds rest and hunt as a group, and fly together from one feeding area to another.

A spoonbill sleeps and rests standing on one leg.

egrets

spoonbills

storks

How do you think spoonbills
use the trees in a swamp?

13

It's Time to Build a Nest

In spring, male and female roseate spoonbills form pairs.

The male spoonbill collects sticks.

The female uses the sticks to build a large nest in a tree.

Once the nest is ready, the female lays one to five eggs in it.

a male spoonbill collecting sticks

The parent spoonbills take turns sitting on the eggs to keep them warm.

nest

Baby Spoonbills

About three weeks after the eggs were laid, the baby birds hatch.

The mother and father must feed their hungry babies.

The parent birds gobble up lots of fish, shrimp, and insects.

Then they spit up the food into their chicks' bills.

Newly hatched spoonbills are born with wet feathers. Their feathers, called down, soon dry and become fluffy.

fluffy down

egg

newly hatched chick

Hold a tennis ball in your hand. The ball weighs about 1.8 ounces (51 g). That's how much a newly hatched spoonbill chick weighs.

a parent spoonbill feeding a chick

Dangers in the Swamp

At two weeks old, the chicks start to explore outside the nest.

However, the spoonbills have to keep an eye out for **predators** in the swamp.

Raccoons and birds, such as hawks, hunt and eat young chicks.

Alligators and bobcats attack spoonbill chicks and adults.

mother spoonbill

two-week-old chick

hawk

Predators such as raccoons and snakes eat roseate spoonbill eggs.

raccoon

alligator

19

All Grown Up

At six weeks old, a roseate spoonbill chick has lost its fluffy down.

It's covered with white feathers, and the bird can now fly.

It takes about two years for a spoonbill's feathers to turn pink and red.

At three years old, a roseate spoonbill is all grown up.

Now it's ready to find a partner and have chicks of its own!

father spoonbill

six-week-old spoonbill chick

The shrimp that an adult roseate spoonbill eats contains substances that turn the bird's feathers pink.

Think of a new name for the roseate spoonbill that describes how it looks or how it lives.

Science Lab

A Bird's Life

There are hundreds of different types of birds in the United States.

Choose a bird that lives in your neighborhood and then use books and the Internet to research how it lives.

Next, make a chart like the one shown on the right to compare and contrast the life and habitat of a roseate spoonbill with the bird you've chosen.

Roseate Spoonbills and Cardinals

Things that are the same:	Things that are different:
Both birds have wings and can fly.	Spoonbills often live in swamps, while cardinals often live in backyards.
Spoonbills and cardinals both lay eggs.	Spoonbills eat fish and shrimp. Cardinals eat seeds and fruit.

roseate spoonbill

northern cardinal

Science Words

bill (BIL) a bird's beak

predators (PRED-uh-turz) animals that hunt other animals for food

shallow (SHAL-oh) not very deep

swamp (SWAHMP) a wetland habitat where trees and bushes grow from the water-covered land

wading (WAYD-ing) walking through water or mud

wetland (WET-land) a habitat where the land is covered with shallow water; plants grow from the water-covered land

Index

Read More

Cooper, Sharon Katz. *Marshes and Pools (Horrible Habitats).* Chicago: Raintree (2010).

Dayton, Connor. *Wetland Animals (American Habitats).* New York: PowerKids Press (2009).

Person, Stephen. *Roseate Spoonbill: Pretty in Pink (America's Hidden Animal Treasures).* New York: Bearport (2013).

Learn More Online

To learn more about roseate spoonbills, visit **www.bearportpublishing.com/SwampThings**

About the Author

Ellen Lawrence lives in the United Kingdom. Her favorite books to write are those about nature and animals. In fact, the first book Ellen bought for herself, when she was six years old, was the story of a gorilla named Patty Cake that was born in New York's Central Park Zoo.

McLEAN MERCER REGIONAL LIBRARY
BOX 505
RIVERDALE, ND 58565

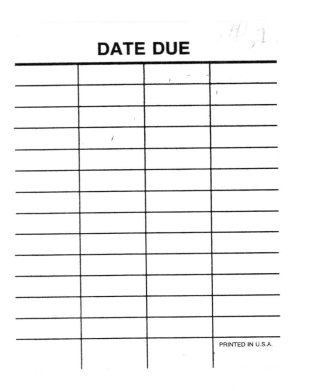

DATE DUE

PRINTED IN U.S.A.

DISCARDED